JN069567

For Happy Life

Edited by
Nihon Shitsuke-no Kai

For Happy Life

Edited by Nihon Shitsuke-no Kai

Translated by Yutaka Karasawa

Fuzambo International

For Happy Life

The first edition on 6th November, 2020

Editor : Nihon Shitsuke-no Kai

Translator : Yutaka Karasawa

Publisher : Kikko Sakamoto

Publicatoin : Fuzambo Internationl Ltd.

　　　　　1-3 Kanda-Jimbocho, Chiyoda-Ku,
　　　　　Tokyo, 101-0051, Japan
　　　　　TEL ＋81-3-291-2578　FAX ＋81-3-219-4866
　　　　　URL www.fuzambo-intl.com

Printing : Fuzambo International Ltd.

Bookbinding : Kato Seihon Ltd.

ⒸNihon Shitsuke-no Kai, Yutaka Karasawa

　2020 Printed in Japan

　　　　ISBN978-4-86600-089-3 C0012

Table of Contents

2. School

3. Society

4. Nature

To children and adults who read this book:

It has just entered into the 21st century that you are living now. The century before that, the 20th century, was a time when science and technology had developed tremendously. Many things have been born and created one after another and it has become a very convenient world.

Certainly, the 20th century was a hundred years when machines changed the way people lived. There were two big wars in the world and many people died. And the industrialized society destroyed nature and left a big impact. Thanks to material civilization, society has become richer, the economy has expanded, and the lives of people have been extended. But on the other hand, people who suffer from mental sickness have been increased.

As one of the countries that caused World War II, Japan continuously has been demanded from the world to reflect on what we have done during the war. Therefore, there are many things that we have to take responsibility and change. However, there are some areas where it has gone too far and has become timid. One of them is our mind.

Due to Japanese collapse after World War II, the way the family live has changed completely in Japan. We often studied by incorporating many influences from the world. The way a family used to live in the same house for three generations has changed to the individual oriented and only the core family members live together that became more common and each has their own private room. So, Japanese traditions that have been kept long time were lost.

The country we live in, unlike other countries, Japan has a history of 2,000 years. The long and good tradition of 2,000 years has accumulated from parents to children and children to grandchildren. And we acquired them unconsciously. We have been transferred "Shitsuke (discipline)" that all Japanese people should have in our mind for the basics of beautiful way of life.

However, it is now difficult for even a family that is a smallest unit of society to maintain good traditions and to transfer because of various changes. And without thinking about our mind, a society was built up in what money, goods, convenience, and speed are priorities. And the economy expanded significantly, but our lives are poor and our society is lonely with less original Japanese mind.

Looking back now, who is responsible for letting it so? At

least, it's not the responsibility of yours, "children".

Oh! Oya (Parents)? Hey?

Yes, we "parents" are responsible. We "parents" have a great deal of thought and reflection on what we have done, and we are looking forward very much on yours to own the future society.

By all means, we would like you as a Japanese to change the course and do your best for the world with rich mind as a human being.

At the beginning of the Constitution with 17 Articles established by Prince Shotoku 1400 years ago, there is a saying, "Harmony is the most valuable thing". These words are the very source of "Shitsuke (discipline)", we think. The heart of the Prince is principle of big harmony, "Yamato-mind", which requires us to serve an individual for a family, a family for a country, and a country for the world.

We hope that Japan in the future will be a rich country in terms of both mind and goods. It may be the time for the whole Japan to re-start human education by returning to its initial intention as Japanese. We would like to ask parents and children or seniors and children to read this book together and discuss.

1. Home

Do you know the word "Shitsuke (discipline / good-manner / etiquette)"?

We think everyone has heard the word "Shitsuke (discipline)" if you are Japanese. Then, do you know what kanji to write? We write "Body to be beautiful" and read it "Shitsuke".

Most kanji came far from ancient China, but "Shitsuke" is different. This is a kanji that was born in Japan and is called "Kokuji (national character)".

Let's take a closer look at the character "Shitsuke".

It's written that "oneself" is "beautiful". Since "oneself" is the body, it means making oneself to be beautiful both physically and mentally is "Shitsuke".

But it's not about dressing nicely or building up your body smartly at a gym. By practicing repeatedly, it is natural to learn beautiful behavior and standing-sitting behavior that everyone evaluates. Furthermore, through the practice, to polish up the invisible heart naturally to be beautiful.

You learned from your teacher how to keep your movement of feet and hands together during marches such as athletic meet. Wouldn't it be beautiful to see a march that the movements of all were lined up together? Marching is "Shitsuke" as a group to act together with everyone in the same mind.

But before that, "Shitsuke" as a person is important. When you meet someone, look at eyes each other and greet them. When greeting politely or thanking, bow properly, you should look at the other person's eyes first, then bow and raise your head and look at the eyes again. When eating meal, use chopsticks correctly and do not make noise. Do not put your elbows on the table during meals. We believe that you have taught such "Shitsuke" from your parents and adults since you were small.

People who are "disciplined" have beautiful behavior and make people around them feel good. If people are not "disciplined", they tend to be selfish and themselves are more important than others. Above all, they wouldn't have friends with beautiful hearts.

Now in Japan, people who haven't been "disciplined" even after becoming adults are gradually increasing. When that happens, our society will be getting worse more and more.

This book was written to stop it. Let's think in your daily life what it means making yourself to be beautiful. Please read this book as many times as you like until the end.

Let's place the shoes properly at the entrance

When you enter into someone's house, do you align your shoes after taking off? It is a basic Japanese Shitsuke to enter into the house by aligning your shoes after taking off. By doing that,

"I can do everything by myself properly"

"I know the importance of settlement"

"I know the meaning of aligning"

It will lead to such things.

But that's not enough.

When you align your shoes after taking off, if other people's shoes are left there as they were after taking off, align them without telling anything to anyone.

Don't say, "Oh, someone is leaving theirs after taking off. They should not do." All you need is to align them. You can do it in a second.

How is the entrance of your house?

Are the shoes of your family cluttered?

If so, you are on duty from today. As a person in charge of aligning shoes at the entrance, let's align everyone's shoes. Tell your father and mother, "I was told to align my shoes at school, so I will take care of my house." Then, everyone will come to own it.

The entrance is the face of the house. If people find it clean, they will understand that the other rooms, baths and kitchens are thoroughly cleaned.

Having all the shoes at the entrance are aligned, people who visited the house feel good.

They understand "Oh, this house is decent".

Not only that but also the hearts of the whole family will be a little more beautiful. This is because if you look at things that are not disturbed or that are aligned, your heart will be affected and you will be beautiful.

If your family has a lot of quarrels, you may have a little less quarrels.

If you always keep your shoes aligned after taking off, it will become a habit over time.

When you go to other houses or shops, you will naturally become a person who will come in after aligned your shoes.

Then, the other person recognizes that you are decent person. In that way, it's also very important to have an eye to notice the appearance of a decent person.

It is embarrassed that not recognizing even if it's aligned or not noticed even it's clean up. Let's do things decently and notice them. Increasing such people is one of the ways to improve our society.

The early bird gets the worm

The old people recommended that we should get up early in the morning, saying that "Early risers stand to gain three mon (early bird gets the worm)". Nowadays it is different from the old days and there are more adults working in the middle of the night. Still, there are many people who keep getting up early.

Why should we get up early? There are many reasons.

The first is that "it is best for humans to work with the sun". Humans have been acting with the sun for tens of thousands of years. In the morning, when the sun rose, they got up and went out for hunting, field work, or fishing by boat. Then in the evening they came home and prepared to rest.

It is only a few hundred years ago that humans have invented lights such as lamps and light bulbs so that they can live at night the same as daytime. Therefore, the human body has a solid mechanism for living with the sun. The life of waking up until late at night and sleeping until noon is a way of life contrary to that mechanism. There are many people who get sick in bodies or hearts because of that.

The second is a practice to control your selfish mind. When you wake up in the morning, there aren't many people who don't think "Oh, I'm sleepy. I want to sleep more". Everyone loves easy and comfortable things. However, if you do with your desire, you will lose your tense of heart & body and become a sloppy person.

Every person who decided to "get up early every day" has to fight with their desires every morning. And by winning that battle, your mind and body will become tense.

The third is because it is more efficient to get up early to study or work. There are often elder brothers and sisters who say, "I spent the night studying all night" but it's not good for their bodies to study without sleep.

Rather than that, it's much easier to set a time to study and wake up early. If you look closely, people who stay up all night often sleep more during the day.

By the way, how much money is the "three mon" of old

people? Probably it is about 100 yen now. You might think, "Well, that's it?" However, if you earn 100 yen each day, it will be 36,500 yen in one year, and more than 360,000 yen in 10 years.

To put it the other way around, since you just get up early and gain little by little every day, so on the other hand, you might say that "morning sleep is a loss".

Let's become a person who can use chopsticks properly

Can everyone use chopsticks properly when eating?

If you are wondering, "How is mine?", ask the adult person. However, recently, adults who cannot use chopsticks properly are increasing so that it may be necessary to choose the right person to listen to.

Some people call Japanese as "People from the country of chopsticks". Of course, there are countries other than Japan, such as China and South Korea that use chopsticks also. But there are no countries to use chopsticks with more detail manner and many types of chopsticks than Japan. There is a "chopstick culture" in Japan.

Someone might think, "It's a pain to use chopsticks. We can use a fork and a spoon." However, there are no tools than chopsticks that are more suited for Japanese meals and the characteristics of Japanese people.

For example, Japanese people are said to be good at hands. They are good at folding complex Origami and assembling small machines. About fifty years ago, Japan sold TVs and cars to all over the world to enrich the country. And it is said that was helped very much since Japanese are good at hands.

The reason why Japanese are good at hands is thought because we were trained by using chopsticks from an early age. We were taught to pick up a piece of rice one by one with chopsticks to clean up the rice bowl, we were able to do detailed work from the time we were children.

And, the meal with chopsticks is often beautiful in the form. Even when you eat lined in a narrow space, you can eat without having your arm collide with your neighbors. If this were a knife and a fork, that wouldn't be the case. The appearance of eating meals using chopsticks is related to Japanese culture such as Ikebana (flower arrangement) or Sadoh (tea ceremony).

One more thing, when you can use your chopsticks correctly, people around you will evaluate that "That child is properly disciplined", "Maybe the child growing up in a family whose father and mother are decent", "The child must have been studying hard at school" they say.

It is not good to decorate yourself with lies, but it is not bad to show the truth. Use your chopsticks properly and let others around you know that you are a proper Japanese child.

Do you say "Itadakimasu (Let me eat)"?

When we have meals, we say "Itadakimasu". This is normal for Japanese people. However, the number of people who say "Itadakimasu" at any time is gradually decreasing. For example, what about your home?

It is common for Japanese people to say "Itadakimasu", but it is not easy to explain the meaning of this word to overseas people. The word "Itadakimasu" is polite word of "Morau (get)", but what do we get when eating?

The answer is that the words "I am grateful" to tell the honest feeling of "thanks giving to me" for blessing of nature and for the results of the efforts of many people. Meat and fish, rice and wheat, and a variety of vegetables are all blessing of nature.

For example, if the letter of "rice" is apart, it looks like "eight-ten-eight (eighty-eight)". Old people told to their children that "It takes 88 times of tasks to make rice". That's how parents instructed their children not to waste even a single piece of rice.

We can eat without any special effort because there were some people who made, carried, processed and cooked the ingredients. We cannot forget how grateful they are.

"Thank you" to both your immediate parents and those who are not visible. That is the "Itadakimasu" before starting meals.

Furthermore, don't forget that all foods are "lives". Not only meat and fish, but plants are also living things. In order for us to live, we must always receive the lives of other creatures and eat them.

In order to live, we have to get another life. In response, we say "I'm sorry, thank you" and we say "Itadakimasu".

There are some adults in the restaurants and cafeterias who do not say "Itadakimasu". The reason is "I don't express my gratitude because I'm paying money." But how do you think about this idea?

You already understand, don't you? To have life and to thank the person who prepared the food is necessary but not "un-necessary" because we paid the money.

Actually, if there is a war or a major disaster, food may not be available regardless of any amount of money. If you think that money is the most valuable thing, nobody may help you when you get stuck.

After the meal, we say "Gochiso-sama (Thanks for the meal)"

When we finished the meal, we would say "Gochiso-sama (Thanks for the meal)", but these words are not good enough just saying aloud.

"Gochiso-sama" is the word "chiso (feast)", which means running around and doing something, with the polite words "go" and "sama".

The old days unlike now, we couldn't easily buy foods at stores, so when customers visited us, we ran around and gathered the ingredients to make them eat delicious meal. You might have run a horse farther, sailed out into the sea, or gone into the mountains.

The word "Gochiso-sama" is an expression of gratitude for their actions and sincerity. If you look carefully, there are some people who put hands together when saying "Gochiso-sama", but it is a natural gesture that expresses gratitude.

By the way, when we say "Gochiso-sama", there is a courtesy that we must follow. That is we eat everything on our plates cleanly.

Nowadays there aren't many people to pay attention to, but in old days, adults scolded children when they left some meals on their plates.

For example, if a child found some grains of boiled rice on the lid of a lunch box then a child who is well brought up will eat them cleanly with chopsticks.

It became the courtesy that such an attitude not to waste the food, to eat them all cleanly and to respect the heart of person who made the food,

There is not enough food in the world now. In Japan, half of food is thrown away due to leftovers, expiration date and so on, but in some areas of the world, there are many people who die without food.

Even though your country has enough money and rich it does not mean that you can waste food. Reflections have begun in other countries around the world, and in Germany in

22

Europe, for example, left over meal at a restaurant costs € 1 penalty. In time, it may happen in Japan.

Leaving food is a bad thing. Now you understand, don't you?

Do by yourself what you can

"Let's do by yourself what you can do." You often hear this phrase don't you? When we were little, everything was done by our father, mother, and people around us, but as we grow older, we have to do it by ourselves. "It would be easier if someone could do for me", "Why do I have to do it by myself?"Have you ever thought that way?

But doing what you can do is the minimum rule for living as a child. At least, children don't earn money or make meal. Adults do such important things, so at least children should do as much as they can.

When becoming an adult, humans cannot live on their own. You have to work for life and for someone else rather than yourself. The older a person is, the more they use their life for others.

There is another reason that you have to do what you can. It is a training to increase "what you can do". You can already fold your clothes, clean up a messy room, and do simple cleaning, don't you?

Then, can you go one step further to put the folded clothes into the closet, to clean up the other rooms of the house, or to help a little difficult cleaning?

The cleaning the floors or wiping the windows could be considered as the time for physical education and move your body as much as possible. Then, the meal will be deliciously eaten and you will be getting energetic.

As new things become possible, the human brain is ready to feel joy. And you would like to do more and more new things. People who do more can work smarter than those who do less. And that feeling can be applied not only to various things in life, but also to study and exercise.

There are people around you who are good at studying even though they don't seem to study a lot. There should be people who can do well in physical education on whatever they do. They were not different since they were born but they knew the fun of increasing what they could do.

If you feel like "It's troublesome would not someone do for me?" please remind what described above.

The importance of organizing and aligning

Your family members and teachers often say, "Clean up!" don't they?

Don't you think "I understand, I'll do it later" each time?

However, the easiest and most fun way to clean up is to "do it right away". The more you extend it later, the much harder, painful and unpleasant it will be to clean up.

By the way, why should we clean up?

The reason is that if you don't clean it up, it becomes difficult to use the room and tools.

For example, an old Japanese house used to live in tatami rooms. There were no beds, no tables, no furniture, but only cabinets.

When we woke up in the morning, we folded the futon mattress and put away into the closet. Then, we brought out a low table called Chabudai that the legs could be folded, and laid the tableware on it, and ate breakfast.

After we finished breakfast, we removed the tableware and put away the table. When the children came home from school and do their homework, they would bring out the Chabudai again. As such, one room became a dining room, a living room, a play room, a study room, or a bedroom.

In this way, the old Japanese used the narrow house widely and wisely. For that, the clear away after doing things every day was very important.

Nowadays, there are dining rooms, living rooms, bedrooms, and child rooms that are all dedicated rooms. So you can eat meals or sleep with leaving the toys out and even without cleaning up. However, if you leave things out, someone may trip over and fall down or break things. We are particularly worried because Japan is the country of earthquakes.

It is said that the brain works better if you clean it up. You will be better at handling things and less likely to break things. You will be able to get a better idea of what is where so that if you would have a typhoon, an earthquake, or a power outage, you will not be difficult to find out something.

And the most important thing is that the more you can clean up, the better you can study and work. Therefore, a person who is good at cleaning up will be assigned an important task or a responsible role after grown up to an adult.

It seems that some people or companies intentionally let to clean up to judge if the person is capable or not. At work or cooking, it is often said the words "well organized" among adults. We call people so who set a beginning and end, and who can see into the future.

We want to be able to clean up by ourselves before someone tells us "Clean it up!". You can do it.

Be a person who cares about your parents, grandparents, senior people and ancestors

Have you ever been to the "grave visit"?

On the spring and autumn equinox days and each anniversary of death, the parents used to visit the grave with their children. When it has been a habit since childhood, it is said that after becoming an adult, it becomes a person who cares about parents and ancestors. On the other hand, it seems that people who have grown up without that habit will not visit the grave and will not care about their parents.

But why is it important to visit the grave? The reason is that by having the idea of "value the origin", you can naturally say "thank you" to various things. Every creature has parents. A child is born from parents and that continues to the grandchild. There is no single exception. Of course, humans are the same. Even if they aren't there right now, you all have a father, a mother, and 4 grandfathers and grandmothers.

The grandfather and grandmother have 8 great-grandfathers and great-grandmothers, and on top of that, there are 16 great-great-grandfathers and great-great-grandmothers.

In this way, going back all the way, there are more than 1,000 ancestors in the 10th generation. It is one million people back in the 20th and one billion people back in the 30th.

How do you think? Don't you think it's a great number?

Even if only one of them was missing, you could not be born into this world. If one of the ancestors of the 30th generation back was prematurely dead, 29th was not born then 28th nor 27th and this way it could be end up the chain of ancestors.

Among many of your ancestors, some of them would have nothing to eat and no place to live in times of war or crops were poor due to bad weather. Now you are here since they had been desperately living.

There is an event called relay in the athletic meet and we can think that it is connecting life baton like relays. That's why we truly need to say "thank you" for the people who connected the baton.

Don't think it's "Atarimae (as usual)"

There are people who complain about various things immediately. Even if the train is a few minutes late, the station staff will be bellowed, and when the restaurant is slow to serve meals, the staff will be bellowed. When the children are playing, they will be told their voices are too noisy, and when senior people are slow to cross the path, they will be horned informing faster walking.

What all of these people have in common is the mind that everything should be "Atarimae". They think that the train moves on time as usual, the food comes out immediately at the restaurant as usual, the usual products are sold at the usual price at the supermarket as usual, the quiet surroundings are common around their houses, and the pedestrians are natural to cross the road quickly.

But is this idea correct?

Actually, there is no such thing as "Atarimae" in this world. Have you ever been told by teachers and family members not to use the word "absolute"? Just as there is almost no "absolute" in this world, there is almost no "Atarime".

There is a reason to write "almost" here. Because there

is only one thing that it should happen always. That is "A person once born who will die in some day absolutely". That is the only thing that happens absolutely and is usual matter. However, other than that, there is no absolutely and no usual.

To control a train running without one minute delay is much harder than we think. Not only drivers and conductors, but also station staff, people on track maintenance, people in garages, people at the driving command center, etc. all these staff of the railway company are doing their assigned jobs properly thus it was realized.

Even so, if the train breaks down, there is an accident at the railroad crossing, or if there is a medical emergency, the train will be delayed. Then the people of the railway company desperately try to get back to the right condition.

Then, what would you feel if you were blamed "Oh inexcusable, why it's late?" You may feel regretful or disappointed.

There is no "Atarimae" in the world. We want to get into the habit of thinking about people who are working hard in places we can't see.

If you are going abroad with your father and mother, please go and see the hard country where people live desperately.

You can understand how good Japan is. When you face with such a scene, you will surely be a kind person.

"Yokubari (Greedy mind)" is the beginning of unhappiness

Have you ever seen the news of "trash house" on TV news shows or other media?

It's a story that when senior person who lived alone got sick, staffs of the public office went into that house to help, things and garbage were piled up, and there was no place for foot. It is said that the foods went bad and often emit bad smells.

Why would that happen? For one thing, it seems that people aged, their bodies work poorly and don't have the energy to clean things up. However, not all senior's houses that live alone are trash houses.

Perhaps those senior persons were not good at cleaning up since they were young. They might not be able to do anything by themselves because they have been storing things up one after another.

A person doing brain research says, "If I look at a person's room, I can imagine the brain condition." If the house is not tidy, it means that the inside of head is also not tidy. There is another way to say that a person, who can't keep things organized and tidy, will not be able to do a good job.

One of the causes of storing things is "greedy mind". Even it is not really needed, they wanted this and that, gather things around them, and they don't give it to anyone even it is not required actually saying that it is "wasteful" or it is "useful". Since they don't give it away to the people who need, they pile up things.

However, it is not the proper way of life of human beings to live being surrounded by things. Human beings are born naked and die without having anything. Only memories of what kind of person and how lived will be left.

"Greedy mind" makes their heart dark and narrow. Since they don't want to be taken away what they have, they will suspect other people. Worse thing is that there is no limit to the "greedy mind" heart. It makes them to want more and more that might become the purpose of life.

The target of "greedy mind" is not only the things but also

money. If that happens, even if you have money, your life will not be happy.

Let's value all lives

Japan is called "Suicide country" alongside its neighbor, Korea. Looking at the world ranking of the suicide rate per capita, Korea is ranked first and Japan is ranked second in developed countries.

In Japan, as many as 34,000 people died of suicide in 2007. The numbers are slowly declining, reaching to 24,000 in 2015, but still it is the number one cause of death for people in their 20's and 30's.

There are many ways to think about why Japanese people commit suicide so much. Unlike Christianity and Islam, Japanese religions such as Buddhism and Shinto do not prohibit suicide. It is also mentioned that there was a method to protect the honor by suicide called "Seppuku (harakiri)" during the samurai era. When the samurai died by harakiri, the woman followed him with a suicide called "Jigai (kill oneself)".

Japanese women may even commit suicide by such as

entering into a waterway or jumping into a railroad, with their children on the way, but these behaviors are wondered from abroad.

Suicide is not the correct way to use life. To live correctly means to use your valuable life that are given and use your valuable body, and do your best to do what you want and to benefit others.

From the view of people who still want to live but who cannot live because of illness or the like, it is egoistic and selfish behavior to end up the life by thinking "all over".

Even if suicide is an extreme example, there are many people in our society who do not care about their bodies. Some people spend their days by drinking a lot, by playing around until late at night because they are young and healthy. Some people who drive cars and motorcycles at dangerous speeds because that are thrilling and fun. Some people do not go to the hospital although in sick because they think they are OK.

Another thing that has been increasing is an accident due to a violation of bicycle manners. They don't care about other people but they only care themselves, they injured the other person by speeding up a narrow road or jumping out at an intersection. This can be said to be a life-threatening action. Driving a bicycle while using a cell phone and holding an umbrella is also very dangerous.

It may be good to ask a police officer to hold seminars at the school yard frequently to learn proper bicycle manners.

People who despise their lives are those who don't care about themselves. A person who doesn't value oneself cannot value others. In other words, even though you are born as a human being, you have lived your life with irresponsible and without concern. There is nothing more wasteful in this world than this way.

Please do not be that kind of person.

Let's do the followings; go to bed early at night, take enough sleep, get up early in the morning, eat breakfast, and exercise energetically to bring your body healthy, don't hate any meals, take snacks moderately, don't do any dangerous actions, and think about safety of yourself and others'.

If you live with above ways, surely wonderful things are waiting for you.

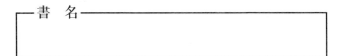

小社の出版物はお近くの書店にてご注文ください。
書店で手に入らない場合は03-3291-2578へお問い合わせください。下記URLで小社
の出版情報やイベント情報がご覧いただけます。こちらでも本をご注文いただけます。
www.fuzambo-intl.com

郵便はがき

| 1 | 0 | 1 | 0 | 0 | 5 | 1 |

東京都千代田区
神田神保町一の三 冨山房ビル 七階

㈱冨山房インターナショナル

読者カード係 行

お　名　前		（　　　歳）男・女
ご　住　所	〒	
		TEL：
ご　職　業 又は学年		メール アドレス	
ご　購　入 書　店　名	都道 府県	市郡区	書店
			ご購入月

★ご記入いただいた個人情報は、小社の出版情報やお問い合わせの連絡などの目的
　以外には使用いたしません。
★ご感想を小社の広告物、ホームページなどに掲載させていただけますでしょうか?
【　可　・　不可　・　匿名なら可　】

Let's listen carefully to the story of seniors

The old Japanese house was called a big family, and a big family lived in one house. A great-grandfather, a great-grandmother, a grandfather, a grandmother, a father, a mother, uncles, aunts, brothers, sisters, cousins lived together. Or, there were cases with no great-grandfather and no great-grandmother but with nieces or nephews.

So, in many families with various ages connected by blood, each person had a role that was appropriate. Mostly they were farmers, so powerful people go to the fields to do farm work. When planting and harvesting rice, the whole family work together.

During that time, it was the job of seniors to take care of small children.

Approximately 50 years ago, Japan started to form a small family called nuclear family. A father, a mother and children, or one parent and a child are family members. Due to the increase of such small units, the number of occasions where seniors play their active roles has decreased. With more work to do at offices or factories, it has become more difficult to make money for senior people.

For that reason, there is a mood in Japanese society to treat seniors as obstacles.

However, seniors have the experience of living for a long time. They have many thinking from their long lives. They remember many failures and successes. It's a lot of waste if they do not teach that knowledge and make them useful. Do not you think so?

Now, it would be difficult to bring Japanese society back to large family system. We may be able to do so in the future, but in 10 or 20 years we cannot easily change the society.

Instead, there are things you can do right away. It is for children to hear the story of seniors. Ask your teachers and people in the community to create an opportunity to hear the story of seniors. While listening to the story, keep records in the notebook, write a report later, and make presentations.

It's a good idea to have a day that adults go to nursing homes with their children, push wheelchairs and listen to their stories. For seniors, it seems to live longer if they interact with children. It is said that talking is good for preventing dementia.

Furthermore, in the future, kindergartens and elementary

schools may be in the same building with nursing homes. If the children and the seniors are always in contact with each other, the seniors will get energetic and the children can hear interesting stories. Since seniors love to meet with children, they will talk gladly about interesting stories of different worlds.

2. School

Greeting from you

Do you all can do proper greetings?

You thought, "Of course, I can do that", didn't you?
Then, when you came to school in the morning, did you say "Good morning" to the people who passed by on the road?

Eh! Do you say that you said it for someone you knew? Then, we cannot give a passing score. When you said to the person on the road to school "Good morning" from you, then we can say that "Your greetings were completed properly."

At school, there are signs or cues for greetings, and all say, "Good morning" or "Itadakimasu" together. That's why everyone may think "I can do greetings properly".

However, the basic of greetings is to "greet from you first". And at that time, your eyes have to see the other person's eyes. But don't look at them. If so, the other person will be surprised. After seeing eyes lightly, you say "Good morning" or "Hello", then bow.

  Some people wondered, "Why should I do that?"
  Then, let's try to see how adult people do at work. When
working, adults exchange business cards with their first
partners and bow each other saying, "It's nice to see you."

  Not because it's a job, but because when people meet, they
do greetings. Moreover, if you are exchanging money or
things with the person, you need a more polite greeting.

  People who can't do greetings are not valued in the society.
They would be thought who really care about themselves
so that they can't easily make friends. When they made a
mistake, they would be doubt that it might be on purpose. Not
to be such a person, let's become a person who can do proper
greetings with neighbors from the time of childhood.

Why is "cleaning" important?

  Your school may have a rule called "cleaning duty", right?
  How do you do cleaning with what kind of feeling?

  You might think, "I don't like it. It's dirty, it's tiring, and
there's nothing good about it."
  There are some adults who think that "a person who spe-

40

cializes in cleaning should do this kind of work".

But cleaning is important. There was an oversea TV station who visited to make their news program since the cleaning duty of an elementary school in Japan was wonderful. And they got a big response from viewers that, "Eh? In Japanese schools, do children do their own cleaning just like they do at home?"

The program explained, "In Japanese schools, by having children clean up, they can respect each other and have a sense of responsibility." Even if it's a toilet, they clean up where they did dirty. This will help them to live with care so that they don't have to clean it as much as possible. Being grateful to others when they know someone is doing cleaning where they have been messing around.

But the biggest effect of cleaning is to "brush your mind". Once upon a time, there was a person who went to the temple to practice the mind. The Buddhist monk made the person clean from morning till night. After forced to do cleaning so many days, the person told the monk, "Why do you just force me cleaning?"

The monk said this, "You want to make your heart beautiful, don't you? But you can't take your heart out and brush it. You can only make things that reflect on your mind as beautiful as possible. So you should make everything you see beautiful."

The person was noticed when he heard these words. "Well, was this a practice of the mind? Until now, I had been making a fool of cleaning things. From now on, I will do it with all my heart."

As soon as that person started to think that way, he began to treat people in a kind and polite manner, as if he had changed to another person.

Be a listener more often than a speaker

The word "speaking" is "hanasu" when written in kanji. Do you know other ways of writing? Even if you look up the Japanese dictionary, there is only one letter.

Then how about "hearing"? If you have a dictionary near you, please look it up.
How is it?

You would find "hear", "listen" and "ask", wouldn't you? Depending on the person, these three kanji are used properly. For example, "hear" when it comes in through your ears, "listen" when you keep it in your mind, and "ask" when you are asking for the answer from your side.

Why is there only one letter of "speaking" but three letters of "listening"? It's because listening is more important than speaking. Although you are the only person who can "speak", there are as many people as there are humans. If you understand all languages, there are seven billion people. Even in Japanese only, there are 127 million people.

And "speaking" is about expressing your opinion, so once you've talked everything you're thinking about, there is nothing to talk anymore. However, "listening" is endless. There is no limit to the amount of knowledge and ideas that many people have. You can listen as many as you want. Much more can be gained by hearing than books in the school library.

Above all, listening is the best way to get along with others. People open their minds to people who often listen to them, not people who talk well. Isn't that the same for everyone? Although they are important people who tell you interesting stories, but don't you like someone who listens to you often?

Have you ever heard of grandfather and grandmother? Both grandfather and grandmother had childhood. The stories that you have heard at that time cannot be forgotten even you will grow older, and you can remember the place and scenery when you have heard it.

Listening to a lot of stories not only broadens and deepens your knowledge, but also the size of mind capacity will be larger. This is because you will be able to understand the positions and thoughts of various people, and you will be able to think and imagine people different from yourself. That way, you'll be able to inspire things you didn't think about before, or be able to do things that didn't work.

Everyone, please aim to be someone who can listen well carefully rather than someone who can speak well. The word "has the ear to listen" is meant to be a person who can listen well.

Don't say bad things about others

Have you ever said bad things about others?

We suppose there are few people who say "No!"

Everyone should have once or twice (maybe more) said bad things about others. Even if you didn't mean to do that, you could be lured by the other person, or by just momentum.

How did you feel at that time? Did you really enjoy yourself? Are you happy and excited? Surely it would be different.

On the surface, you may have laughed out loud or your voice became louder, but at the bottom of your heart, you should feel dark and heavy.

When people do what they know "it's really wrong", they always feel that way. After you have repeated it many times, you would get used to it and your heart would be bent. One of those things is to say bad things about people.

On the contrary, let's think from the standpoint of the one who was said badly.

How do you feel when you are told, "You are cheeky even a short kid". It is not because of you to be short. Of course, it's not because of your parents either. There is no one who does not feel sad because of such inborn characteristics for the reason of reproaching. Telling bad thing is also teasing.

What if you were told, "You are arrogant although you are not good at exercise". If you are told what usually you are thinking of, your heart might be get scratched. You want to be a person who can exercise more than anyone, but you were said bad things to abandon it. Teasing is something that should never be done, and in a sense, more cruel thing than violence.

If you have some concerns on someone and you can't stand it, ask a teacher to come in between and tell through the teacher. It's not the right way to relieve your gloom by abusing or backbiting.

And let's think again about whether you really can't be patient or not. At that time, look back at yourself to see if you are not doing the same to other people.

There is a word that has been told since long time ago, "One man's fault is another's lesson." Since everybody does something similar, when you are concerned about someone's behavior, be careful if you are doing the same thing or not and fix it if you do so. That's the teaching.

It will be a good thing to try now.

Let's speak your opinion actively

Sometimes people of oversea countries say, "The Japanese do not say their opinions so that we do not know what they are thinking." It might be what happens because many Japanese people are quiet and they are not good at foreign languages such as English.

Also, since Japanese society is so called "homogeneous culture", it is a group of people who are very similar to each other. That's why people will understand the most of things without explaining actively. For that reason, it seems that there is a habit to rely on others that "No need to say, no."

But overseas societies are not. People are often gathered from various places on the earth so that races, religions, and customs are different. Sometimes, you may not even be able to understand any words. In such a place, no one understands or even not tries to understand unless we explain ourselves actively.

From now on, Japan will be further internationalized. As everyone knows, the world has become very small with mobile phones and the Internet. People born in overseas may come to work in Japan or marry Japanese and live in Japan. If that happens, the society of being able to understand without talking will be changed.

Even not so, in order to play an active role in the world by leaving from Japan, it is necessary to acquire common sense of the world. So, we hope that everyone should actively speak out own opinions. At that time, it should be careful not to talk about yourself unilaterally, but to talk by thinking about how the other person thinks and if understands what you are talking about. If you talk to the other person without care, it may not convey what you want to say at all. Then it is a waste of time for both.

If you do not say your opinion, the other person will imagine what you are thinking. "Not thinking about anything?", "Judging me stupid and deliberately quiet?", "Thinking to go back early?"

Before you get ridiculous misunderstanding, let's say your opinion clearly. Also, let's make your effort to be able to teach about Japan's four seasons, Sumo wrestling, animation video etc.

For what are you studying?

Why are you studying at school every day?

Is it "to become a good adult"?

Is it "to enter a good school, join to a good company, and have a good life"?

Is it "because parents and teachers say study"?

Is it "because it's fun to know new things"?

Any of these answers are not wrong.

It's hard to understand saying "a good adult", but it may be a solid person that is respected by others. To be that kind of person, you should know a lot of things, rather than know nothing.

"Entering a good school, joining to a good company, and living a good life" is the way of thinking in old days of your parents, grandfathers, and grandmothers. Even still now in Japan, it is said that graduates of schools that everyone knows have an advantage over schools that no one knows when taking a company entrance examination.

But it will disappear gradually. It's because the companies become more concerned about "what they can do" and "whether they have beautiful minds", rather than "what kind of school they graduated". Also, in order to do business with world companies, entrance examinations may be conducted at different times, rather than having all the 4th grade students at the same time.

"Try it before think about it." is often a good way to tackle something you don't understand. You just have to try it then continue if you have fun or find your own reason.

"It's fun to know something new" is true for adults. Actually, people with this reason can continue their studies most easily. The human brain has a character of being willing to do fun things, so people who enjoy studying can continue to study as much as they want. Everyone, please find the fun of studying and like it.

For what do you do physical training?

People who are not good at physical education think, "I don't need physical education". "I cannot become an athlete, why do I have time for physical education?"

Please think about the Kanji. "Physical education" means nurturing the body. For musicians, scientists, politicians and scholars, their bodies are the most important. Therefore, in order to make a good body, anyone who will be in any profession in the future will do physical education.

What if while a child decide, "This child will be an astronaut," and only studies to help the astronaut job? Astronauts live in zero gravity so that the physical fitness is one of the conditions.

At elementary school and junior high school, everyone learns in a way that is useful for people without bothering others, regardless of what kind of adult they are. From senior high school students, the direction seems to be getting clearer what they want to do so they will study according to it, and the course will be divided more finely at the college. In the past, they have been studying for everyone like that.

However, physical education is a little different. In physical education classes at elementary and junior high schools, you will not only exercise according to your body during the growing period, but also learn team play that you can only experience in sports. No matter how hard one person works, they learn that they can't beat those who are well organized team, and they learn the essence of organizational activities. Physical education has such a role.

Recently, an accident in gymnastic formations continued, and schools prohibiting gymnastic formations increased. However, the wrong thing was the wish of the teacher who challenged the unreasonable height to make a record, and the gymnastic formations itself is not bad. Gymnastic formations are the sports that even small teams can find rewarding if the height meets the body of the children.

Recent studies have shown that children who have the influence of games and do not exercise enough to play outside often have problems with their mental development. Along with not enough sleep, no breakfast, sitting up late, and lack of nutritional balance, lack of exercise can be harmful to the health of children.

Even if you are not good at exercise, let's play outside actively and move your body.

Let's learn new things starting from "Kata (style/form)"

Traditional Japanese performing arts such as Noh, Kabuki, and Kyogen are said to begin with the learning of "Kata (patterns)". There is no explanation such as "Why you have to do that?", but just remember the basic Kata. It is also copying who succeed it.

This is the same for Sado (tea ceremony), Kado (flower arrangement), Judo, Kendo (Japanese fencing), and Kyudo (Japanese archery), and you will repeatedly practice up to the level where the body moves without thinking about the determined "Kata".

This is quite different from the Western style of teaching, "Teach the reason and after understood then go ahead". There seems to be a backlash that "it's just an old style". But over the long years, that style hasn't changed.

The reason is that learning "Kata" is a fast way to acquire advanced experience in a short period of time. The movement of the human body is controlled by the part of the cerebellum, but it takes time to remember the movements in the cerebellum. It may take many years to do things while thinking its logics. However, if you simply practice repeatedly without any thought, the cerebellum will remember its movements and automatically your body moves.

The old Japanese didn't know academics such as brain physiology, but they knew it only by experience.

Assuming that everyone knows the word "Manabu (learn)",

but did you know that "Manabu" came from "Manebu (imitating)"? Learning is imitating.

In the world of Noh, Kyogen, and Kabuki, the terms "Shu(guard)," "Ha(break)," and "Ri(separate)" are used. The first step to start learning is "Shu", that is to imitate the movements of the teacher and acquired it. Once you have mastered it, the next step is "Ha". They move from basic to advanced steps. Little by little, they will try to break the learned patterns. The last is "Ri", and based on the memory of the cerebellum, you create a unique Kata according to your own thoughts.

When you start a new study, please remember this "Shu, Ha, Ri". And even if your teacher tells to practice the basic patterns repeatedly, don't think it is "uninteresting" or "boring".

Nothing in the world can be very successful if you don't have the basics. As long as we live, studying is necessary at any age. Both of your father and mother started a new study when you were born. We call it "Ikuji(childcare) is ikuji(self-education)".

Don't use violence

At any school, the teacher always says, "Do not use violence". Why is that?

The answer is, "If using violence is forgiven, it will become an animal world."

We assume that you've heard the word "Jaku-niku-kyo-shoku (law of the jungle)".

For example, in the sea, there is a chain relation that plankton is eaten by krill, krill is eaten by small fish, small fish is eaten by large fish, and larger fish eats large fish. That is a law of the jungle. There is no such thing as "it's sad" or "understand by talk". But it is a world of strength in which the strong ones beat the weak ones.

However, since animals know their own social positions by their instinct without taught, they do not have the endless desire as human beings.

On the other hand, human society is different. First of all, humans are not the strongest creatures in nature. The body is smaller than a whale, and its strength is not comparable to a bear. Teeth are weaker than lions and cheetahs run much faster.

Despite that, humans are still living well on the earth because, in part, humans invented tools and used science and technology to do things that other animals could not do. And human beings can do collective actions well, and with the power of numbers, they overwhelmed other animals.

However, in order to fully utilize such human power, it is necessary for the human beings to be able to live together in a group. If, as animals, the strong could let the weak follow by the power, the human society will gradually fall apart. That is why we decided violence to be a "don't do".

Violence is a means for people who cannot solve problems through discussion. Such people are usually selfish and childish. Everyone must warn those who use violence and stop it.

Violence between countries is called "war". A small part of war is "conflict." Conflicts are still irresistible somewhere in the world. In particular, conflicts due to differences in religion are difficult problems to solve. It is necessary to keep saying that "violence should not be done" from countries all over the world without giving up.

Let's respect the "individual personality"

It is often said that "let's value everyone's personality". However, there isn't much explanation about why we have to value individual personality. Why do we need to value individual personality?

To value individual personality is to respect each person's differences.

Because you are different from other people and if you try to remove them or try to fix the differences, it is nothing but erase the good points of the other person.

Human society is a collection of the good points of various people. Once upon a time, the king ruled the country, but no matter how good the king is, he cannot create a society with the goodness of only one person.

Always, the king's shortcomings will be exposed, and the country will weaken from there. Therefore, in order to create a better society, it is important that people with various special characteristics gather together. Gathering more and more people who have special characteristics that are different from other people and creating a group is must.

The person who had made great inventions that were

historic or had changed the lives of people greatly, often had some characters that were very different from other people. Sometimes it was called "stranger" or "eccentric". To try it out, it's good to read the biography of a great historical person that everyone knows. You will understand that the person was a hard worker and also different from others.

The people of that era valued the strange people, so great things in history were done and left. Some of examples you can recognize will be Nobel Prize winners.

So far, in Japanese society, it has been said that it is good to follow the same opinions as everyone else and bad to be different with others. But from now on, we hope each and every one of you to have a firm opinion so that it will be wonderful to understand the difference.

Let's not laugh at someone's special character just because they are different. In addition, let's make your own personality so that you can express your opinion without hesitation.

Do not participate in "bullying"

Bullying is reported daily in newspapers and television

news. There are some people who have been born as human beings and have committed suicide by suffering from bullying, or who have been bullied and cannot go to school. In addition, the person who bullied may be bullied by everyone on the contrary. It was also mentioned in "Do not say bad things of others" on page 43.

Why bullying will not go away? There must be no one in the world who thinks bullying is right. Yet, some people start bullying and others join. A person watching silently is the same as participating in bullying. Won't their hearts get hard?

Actually, the persons who bully are scared. If they are unable to calm their feelings, they will start bullying by finding a suitable person to take their mind off. Most of the time, a person who have a little different characteristics from others will be the target of bullying.

The persons who participate in bullying will fear that they will be bullied next time if they say no so that they join to bullying with fear. They bully others with confidence that they will not be done. This is the chain of evil.

Around them, there are persons who are jeering the bullying by watching like the audience. These persons might think that they aren't involved in bullying, but they are definitely fellow bullies. In addition, some people are quietly watching. Or, there are some persons who haven't seen it but are silent by knowing that there are bullies. These persons may think "we are irrelevant", but they are still fellow bullies.

To the bullied person, these are all enemies, not allies. If there is an ally, it is only the one who is actively trying to stop bullying. If there is no such person in the class, the whole class members will be the enemies. Before this happens, let's help the person together who has the feeling to commit suicide. Let's talk to your parents or teachers.

Bullying is very unhappy whether it is the being done side or the doing side. In order to eliminate such misery from the world, you must never start bullying, join in, or watch quietly.

When humans do what they know to be bad, their hearts become dark and dirty. While repeating it, their hearts will be distorted so much that it is difficult to restore it.

Please make a strong determination that "I will never do anything bad" so that it will not happen.

Let's play well and learn well

Old people said, "Play well and learn well". They knew that it was important not to just learn or play but to balance both. In the previous pages, we mentioned about the importance of physical education.

However, "play" here refers to playing with moving the body in outside. You can play dodge-ball, play tag, or catch insects, but it's not about playing games in a house.

Playing with your body outside will not only train your body, but also reduce the stress of studying. Then the meals will be deliciously eaten and you can sleep well after going to bed. These are very positive effects on your head and body.

Also, playing outside gives the brain a different stimulation from studying that helps to grow the brain.

If you just do playing always without studying since playing outside is good for your brain and body, the other parts of your brain will not grow.

If you don't have enough knowledge and the ability to think, you will struggle to study much higher levels due to lack of the basics.

In other words, studying and playing are like the relation of a main dish and a side dish. By eating both in a well-balanced way, you can maintain your health.

Those who play well and learn well can respond flexibly to things. Playing outside fosters momentary judgment, so you can learn more than just logics but also such as sensations.

And those who play well and learn well have full of ideas. In order to play more interestingly, you have to do not only what you have been taught but also try what you thought and learn from the results.

Recently children have stopped playing outside. Even though the schoolyard is safe, if you're playing at school, you will be told to "go home now", and if you play in the park, neighbors may say "you are noisy". There are no places to play safely because the roads are dangerous due to cars are running. That's why children become only playing games at home. Under these conditions, no matter how many times you are told to play outside, it's not possible. Please tell parents, teachers, and adults if you are in these situations.

It seems that children's exercise amount has fallen to less than a half in the last decade or so. Adults must implement "making places to play and learn well" for their children.

3. Society

Humans are creatures that live in groups

In the primitive age, humans hunted in groups to catch animals larger than themselves and ate them. They already had simple tools, but the biggest weapons were their collective actions, the use of fire, and the superior wisdom over animals.

Since then, humans instinctively try to form groups. When being alone, humans became anxious and lonely so that the brain changed to make their mind unstable. On the other hand, being in a group, they feel happy and relaxed. In other words, humans are animals that instinctively form groups.

After the Iraq war, US military occupied Iraq. Iraqi people have surrounded the US military and were about to jump on. No matter how much they have the latest armaments, they can't match for the number of people. As soon as everyone thought this would get to a serious situation, an American commander ordered the soldiers to "smile!"

Soldiers were surprised, but they smiled at the Iraqi people as ordered. Then, the Iraqi people who were nervous that were relieved and the misunderstandings were resolved. Humans have instinctive mechanism beyond words to be friendly.

The oldest human being was born in Africa. It is believed that they walked from there and spread all over the world, but as human being eventually expanded, they would have met everywhere in the world. If at that time human races were in war, human being may have disappeared sometime in the history.

What is being thought about now is that the primitive people would communicate their thoughts with their gestures, share their food, and soon become friends. That kind of behavior, acting as a group and quickly getting along with other groups, urged the prosperity of humanity today.

People who say "I like loneliness" cannot really live alone. Even if you live in a tent on a mountain, you will live in a tent made by someone and use tools made by someone. If you try to do everything by yourself, it will be very busy every day for just eating and living.

How many times a day do you say "thank you"?

How do you feel when you are told thank you?

Are you happy? Do you feel lightly warm? Do you feel to do something better?

That's right. "Thank you" is a magic word.

Now, how often do you say "thank you" in a day?

How many times did you say at school today?

Did you say "thank you" to your father and mother before you left home?

There are many people around you.

The people are doing a lot of things for you. It is very important to say "thank you" to tell your appreciation for those people.

In the meantime, you will notice.

The people around you were doing various things without knowing them.

Then, even if the other person is invisible, you will feel warm and want to convey your appreciation.

Senior people repeatedly saying "Thank you. Thank you."

in front of the family Buddhist altar is that they are telling to the people who passed away this world and people in the world, a feeling of appreciation for invisible things.

A person who can say "Thank you" genuinely will have broader mind. This is because people in the world can understand that people are relying on "each other". People who only see around themselves can't understand it. So, small things make them angry or worry.

Some people often say, "I don't need to thank you because I paid for it", but that's not the case. It is a rule in the world to spend money when buying things, but if there is a big earthquake or war, you can't buy things no matter how much money you have.

A lot of people who help you in such a case are people who usually say "Thank you".

Don't bother the others

Do you all know the word "Meiwaku (annoyance)"?

"Meiwaku" means that something else causes someone else to feel uncomfortable or get stuck.

For example, when friendly boys are playing with swings

or seesaws in the park, if they occupy these because it is fun, other children who come to play will be disappointed.

Playing in outside with loud voice at late night will wake up people sleeping in nearby homes.

If you talk in the library where everyone is reading books quietly, the people around you will be warned, "Shhh!, be quiet!"

No matter what you do, if you live on a desert island by yourself, you won't bother anyone. However, human beings are living to help each other. So everybody has to care for others to be able to live comfortably.

"Don't bother other people" is a basic rule for that. So at school, you learn collective rules not to bother others.

But lately it has become less executed.

It is because children and adults have become unaware that they are bothering others.

In a crowded train, there are some people who don't notice the sound leaking from their headphones, a woman who is making up on the train because she hasn't had time, and a person who sits on the seat with some extra space than normal space even one more person could sit, a person who are enthusiastic about the mobile phone, sitting in the priority seats, and do not change their seats even when the senior people ride on. Even just a short train ride, it's full of annoyance.

Why has it happened?

One of the reasons is that everyone is not paying attention to each other. Once upon a time when there was a child who bothered someone, an adult who saw it warned to the child, "Don't do that". If doing something bad, a senior person scolded, "No! Stop it!" But without we noticed it, those habits disappeared and the society became not to talk to strangers unless an outstanding thing would happen.

It's not easy to change the habits of the society at once. Therefore, it is important for each person to think, "Don't I bother someone now?" In order to do so, we must think not only from our own standpoint but also have a habit of seeing things from the standpoint of various people.

Let's think about the feelings of the other person. Anyone who thinks "If it's good for me, I'm OK" will not be treated by anyone.

To be a person who keeps promises

"Keeping promises" is one of important rules in our society, but why should we keep promises?

The reason is that in the current society, everyone is supposed to keep their promises.

For example, if the train isn't running on time, we don't know when we should go to the station. An accident may occur if the train does not run as scheduled.

Unless everyone keeps the promise of "stop at the red light," we won't be able to cross the road with peace of mind and there will be traffic accidents everywhere.

If the staffs of post office don't keep the promise that they will "properly deliver the letters they are holding", we will have to deliver the letters and packages by ourselves.

On the contrary if everyone doesn't keep the promise of "trusting the money" we will not be able to do shopping. If we can't use our money, we will be back in the world of bartering at the primitive ages.

In this way, today's human society is made up of all kinds of promises. Therefore, those who do not keep their promises cannot live in the society. You won't be trusted by people, and you won't be assigned to do important jobs. You'll run out of friends and you'll be judged that you are a troublesome person from your family members. If you go to school late or break your promises to friends, no one will associate with you.

There are more important things.

It means that keeping a promise with someone is also keeping a promise with you.

For example, if your teacher said, "Be sure to read this page of the textbook well by tomorrow." And you answered "Yes, I will do." That is one promise.

But you watched TV and went to bed without reading the textbook. Since you thought, "I'm good at reading, so maybe I can read well."

The next day, your teacher told you to read the page in front of everyone. Although you got a little stuck, but you could read better than you expected. "Oh, I was OK." you felt relieved. Because you read it well, you thought you didn't have to keep the promise.

Still it does not have the change that you broke a promise. Your teacher and everyone may not be aware, but your heart knows about it. The promise you broke is a betrayal to your heart. In other words, you are telling a lie to yourself. Such person will not be trusted by other people.

To keep the promise is also to live taking care of you. The idea of "It's OK not to be found" is incorrect.

Why do we keep the "Reigi (courtesy)"?

When you meet a person, you say hello. You use honorifics for superiors in Japan. You bow when it's necessary. In order to live in a society, "Reigi (courtesy)" is necessary in various situations. Why there is "Reigi"? When you meet a stranger, you will be wondering what you should do with the other person. At that time, if the other person greets you in a way you know, you will be relieved and open your mind. "Reigi" can be thought as a rule that allows strangers to get along with each other at ease.

For example, in English-speaking countries such as The United States and The United Kingdom, when you meet someone for the first time, if you say "Hello" or "Hi," and ask to shake hands, and you say "Nice to meet you", you will be recognized that you are a person with whom you can communicate.

It's the same in Japan. If you say that "Hello, it is nice to meet you. My name is such and such. Best regards", you will not be judged to be a strange person. That is the root of Reigi.

Then further it goes, it becomes more complicated Reigi in the complex human relationships. It is said that few Japanese people are able to use Japanese honorifics completely, but it is important to pay attention to the sitting order, greeting order, bow angle, using such honorifics, etc.

But you don't need to feel troublesome. Even if you are not completely performing Reigi, it does not suddenly break your relationships. Reigi is one way to introduce you as "I am this kind of person". When you repeat many times, you will get a sense of decent Reigi and you will be thought, "Oh, this person knows many things". Even if it doesn't happen initially, anyone can see how you are making efforts.

It is said that today's Japanese Reigi method is based on the "Ogasawara-ryu Reiho Hyakkajo (100 methods of Ogasawara Style Reigi)" which was started by Mr. Sadamune Ogasawara, a samurai of the Kamakura era. This book is one of the oldest that was written the word "Shitsuke (discipline)". Today, the Ogasawara-ryu is thought to be learned by women, but it was originally Reigi for samurai in Kamakura. For both men and women, Reigi is important.

The figure of a person who can do either Japanese Reigi or Western courtesy looks very beautiful. Beautiful and lean courtesy & etiquette are very pleasing just to watch. Let's imitate and learn them.

Don't imitate someone doing bad things

There are always people who do bad things both inside and outside of school. Not throwing the trash into the trash can but throwing it around there, or leaving the used ones without settled. The worse ones tell lie without hesitation or don't keep their promises.

Wouldn't you feel like this when you saw someone like that?

"What? Aren't they scolded even they do such bad things. Well then I might be OK if I do?"

"Che, I tried to be a good person and I made an effort but lost. I will stop being a good person."

"Will it be OK even I do bad things if not found?"

To feel that way is understandable but don't copy bad

things.

"Why? Isn't it OK if not found?"

You might think so, but if you do bad things, you will be surely found. Found by whom? Found by yourself.

Also, parents who love their children can tell immediately by looking at their faces when they are doing bad things or lying.

"Even if I was found it, I may not be stood up or scolded."

You may say so, but when you were found by yourself, your heart will be harmed. That is the punishment for doing bad things.

Even if you're doing bad things and your heart was harmed, initially you might think, "Oh, it is not serious". However, your wound heart will gradually feel heavier and darker.

Even if you do something fun, you won't be enjoyable, and even if you want to be happy, you are not happy straightly. That is a very painful thing.

No matter how enjoyable or funny it may be, don't do bad things. Even if you are approached by a good friend, you should clearly say, "It's a bad thing, don't do it."

Doing so, you may help your friends out of the wrong path.

The worst thing is that you don't think well about it and you will be carried away with the people around.

The idea of, "It's OK to do it since my friends do." is very dangerous.

There is a saying that "a red light is not afraid if everyone crosses it", but even if everyone crosses it, to cross the red light is bad thing.

If there is a person who throws away the garbage, nearby person should clean it up. If someone who noticed that the garbage is scattered, cleans it up then no one will throw away the garbage.

Make a line

The most surprising thing for oversea people coming to Japan is that Japanese people line up properly. For example, even in the morning rush hour, they line up properly at the platform and wait still for all the people to get off. It seems that is not the case in other countries in the world. Even in Japan, some regions seem to behave slightly different.

However, even if you run to the door ahead of others, if

there are people in the car, it will only make flustered there. The trains will not be able to leave easily because they will push and react each other. That would just delay the train. The best way is to line up properly and ride on.

In addition, with the launch of new games and so on, enthusiastic fans line up in front of the store for days. Another thing that oversea people are surprised at here is that a stranger properly keeps the order of the person who went to the toilet.

Also, when the Great East Japan Earthquake occurred, people in the disaster area also lined up properly when water and food were distributed. This news traveled around the world and impressed many people, "How polite the Japanese people are, even though there is a danger of life."

This news is not surprising to us Japanese, but they were probably rare for people all over the world. This means, it is said that Japan has fallen apart very much, but it tells that Japan is still a polite country in the world.

Then we should continue to polish our politeness and become a model for the people of the world. It is important to form a line at all times, not to allow cutting in, and to work together for keeping a fair society.

There was a sign like this at an amusement park in The States.

"If you cut in, you will be sent off."

It's a sign that you'll never see in Japan.

We should be proud of being born in such a country.

You are one of them.

Let's keep "Ho-Ren-So (Report-Contact-Consult)"

Have you ever heard the word "Ho-Ren- So"?

It's not one of vegetables, spinach. These are the three important words, "Hokoku (report)", "Renraku (contact)", and "Sodan (consult)", and the words "Ho", "Ren", and "So" are attached together. There was a person who thought an interesting idea, don't you think so?

However, this "Ho-Ren-So" is a very important thing to make the world work well.

If there is no "Ho-Ren-So" in places, not only schools but also where many people work together, such as companies where your fathers work, towns, cities, prefectures, and national governments, they will get into trouble.

For the jobs of making and selling things, it is essential to report the people who are making and selling things.

"Not enough material."

"The machine isn't in good condition, and it's about to break."

"Since the people who are working together are lazy, I'm in trouble."

Such notices can be very important news for those who are watching the whole process. The person can take the necessary steps immediately after hearing the notice.

"The chocolate is sold out."

"Customers told us that on TV, chocolate was good for the body."

"It seems that chocolate-based handmade sweets are in fashion at school right now."

If the notices like these are reported immediately, you may purchase a lot of chocolate and prevent to be sold out.

"Reports" are notifications from bottom to top. For example, at school, the cleaning team reports to the teacher that the broom has worn out. Then the teacher who heard it told the head teacher, "Please buy a new broom," and the news flowed from the bottom to the top.

On the other hand, "Contact" is to inform the side relationship. These include teachers' staff meetings and children's associations.

This is also an important thing like the report, and if you do not contact with others well, you will not know what others are doing. You may do the same thing over and over, or you may do wasteful things without knowing better way.

If your teacher is talking at the staff meeting, "We will make posters for the athletic meet in our class", it will prevent other classes from having made posters.

"Consultation" is to ask various people what you do not understand and what does not work well, regardless of the hierarchical relationship. By asking various people, you may find someone who has similar problems. If you meet someone who know well, you may be able to easily do what you think is difficult.

By consulting, you can let everyone know what you are in trouble now.
Others may take care of you that "that person is busy for that problem now, so let's not ask our favors."

This "Ho-Ren-So" tends to do without paying attention to details if you don't understand your role and feel responsible for it. They report good things right away, but they might hide bad things, or they don't tell important things because it's not interesting that the tasks of others are going well. There will be some people who don't want to be considered as low performers of the tasks, they may not consult to anyone.

These days, at major companies and government offices continue to experience major incidents due to the lack of "Ho-Ren-So". Adults, especially those who are called elites, want to show them great, so it is difficult to keep the rule of "Ho-Ren-So".

Everyone, by all means, be sure to acquire "Ho-Ren-So" surely even from childhood so that you will not become a troublesome adult.

Omoiyari (Thoughtfulness)

There is a word "Omoiyari (thoughtfulness)". The idea is to help people together who are stuck and make the community a better place to live in a town. For a long time, in Japan, mutual help has been widespread through the ideas such as neighborhood associations and circulation boards.

But recently it has changed a little.
"Even if I don't do it, someone will do it."

"Even if I help, I'm sure they won't thank me."

"For those who don't know, it's safer not to get involved."

It is because there are more people who do not try to put their hands on it by saying like above.

Human beings are animals that live in groups, so mutual help is very important. For example, if there are people who were damaged by an earthquake or flood damage, we all need to help them. If you can't go to help, you should help by donations etc.

At the time of the Great East Japan Earthquake, there was a donation of 23.5 billion yen from neighboring Taiwan. It wasn't the money of the country, but it was said to be donated by seniors and children out of their New Year presents. The reason why Taiwanese people cooperated so much was that the Taiwanese seniors remembered that Japanese people used to run city water, made irrigation water, set up train railways, etc. and they have been telling to their children.

However, the world is so complex now and some people pretend to be weak and deceive others. In some countries, if you try to help, their colleagues will come and you will lose your clothes and money. With that in mind, we have to think well not to tell something carelessly.

However, a society without mutual help is unfriendly and

not warm. It must be a few people think that they are happy.

Some people think that helping people is not a good act without a reward, but that is not the case. First of all, helping others makes your heart warm.   And if you are told thank you, you also be impressed by that. Those are enough rewards.

In addition, you can gain various experiences by helping people. It gives you a wider perspective than those who think only about themselves. In other words, you are receiving an invisible reword.

Would you like to help if anyone is in trouble?

It is the mind of thoughtfulness. You have a lot of compassion also, haven't you?

Don't be an arrogant person

There are people in the world who think "I'm special". Because I have a lot of money, I'm the president of the company, so I'm greater than others. They might think like such and become arrogant.

"I'm special, so I can be proud. I don't care about the

feelings of other people". They may be thinking so.

What do people around that person think when they see that figure? Would they think that "that person is great, so it's natural"? Not really. Most of the cases, the person will be thought, "Oh no, unpleasant person."

People who say that they are great because they have a position and have money are only seeing one side of the world. A person who is truly respected is one that people around him/her do not hesitate, even if he/she doesn't say anything. A person who praises and domineers himself/herself is someone who cannot think about his/her long life.

There is a saying, "When the rice plants are more growing, the ears of rice plant are hanging down lower." It means that just like the ears of rice plant are hanging down at a golden rice field that can be seen in autumn, humans will become honest and demure as learning and virtue deepen.

Really fine persons know that "there is no special person in the world". That's why they don't domineer and they know well that the world is "Otagaisama (relying on each other)".

"Otagaisama" is the idea that everyone takes various

positions. Even those who have money now may eventually become poor. Even active and healthy people may someday become sick due to illness.

Everyone who lives in this world has some kind of stress and serious problems, regardless of the difference. And we live beyond those problems.
Thinking so, we should help each other and try to share what we have that is the way to live each other.

If everyone thinks that we are "Otagaisama", the world will be peaceful.

Be a person who evaluate the strengths of others

Have you ever heard the word "dimple search"?

A "dimple" is a dent that will be made on the cheek when a person smiles, but it isn't looking at someone's face. Searching for people's strengths and good points is called "dimple search".

Some people in our society are always complaining. They are always in angry and telling to others "No, no way!" Some of terrible persons, even though they have been talking friendly till now at here, right after standing up the seat, starting to talk others badly.

Those who often talk about bad things of others are good at finding the shortcomings of different people.

"That person soon forgets the important thing."

"That person is just wandering and can't really decide what to do."

"That person is eager to domineer, and only giving directions to others."

These are examples.

However, people like this kind of attitude will not be preferred.

"I suppose this person may be blaming me also."

The person will be doubted as such.

Also, we don't feel good if we keep listening to people's bad words.

Let's say to those people, "Look not for the weaknesses, but for the good points". Every person has disadvantages, but also much strength.

It is interesting that a weakness of one person might be seen as an advantage for another person.

For example, the character that is thought to be "impatient" could be felt "energetic" or "sloppy" becomes "relaxing".

Most people prefer compliment to complaining. Therefore, complimenting strengths rather than saying bad things will be able to make more friends.

If you get angry with someone and you're about to fight, let's try writing good points of the person as much as you can in your notebook. While listing the strengths, the anger will fly away to somewhere.

Let's support those who are making efforts

There is a saying that "You are rewarded if you make an effort", but often hearing the idea that "results are more important than effort". Is the effort important?

The idea that the result is more important than the effort is recent. It is based on the idea of "result-oriented", and for example at your test, it is the idea that regardless of the way of thinking process, you can get points if you have the right answer.

Until then, Japanese society was so called seniority system, and salaries were higher for seniors. However, this is not the case with result-oriented system. What you can do and what you did determines the amount of your salary. As a result, young people may get higher salaries than veterans in some cases.

However, due to the spread of result-oriented system, there are more people who do not care about their efforts. Just give it a try and give up if they couldn't. Then try something else.

But you can't learn something after struggling if you take that approach. Result-oriented people have overlooked it, but the only real blood and flesh of their own is what they get after spending big effort.

The effort is to become a person who wants to do something and who tries as hard as possible by driving own. Sometimes there will be no results even spending big efforts, but if you keep going, you might be able to get it in someday.

When you desperately pursue something that you cannot get easily, various noises will come into your ears.

"No way, it's impossible for you."

"Let's stop because it is a waste of time."

"Since you have no talent, you have no choice but to try something much easier." and etc.

However, it is not good to give up without doing anything.

No matter what, the effort is precious.

There are people who say, "Waste of time," but it's not true. Even if you can't get anything, you still have the reminder that "I continued to make the effort".

So if you see someone making an effort, let's give them support.

Do you know the word "Symbiosis (Living together)"?

In the past, it was thought that the natural world is based on law of the jungle, and only humans help each other. However, as a result of various studies, it has become clear that there is mutual help in the biological world. This is called "symbiosis". It means "living together".

For example, an anemone fish, a type of tropical fish, lives around sea anemones. Sea anemones have poison, and other fishes are numb and eaten by sea anemones, but only anemone fishes cannot be poisoned by sea anemones.

Therefore, the anemone fish, a weak fish, can rest assured that they will not be intimidated by external enemies. On the other hand, anemone fish eat the trash of sea anemone and clean it.

Also, legumes have root nodules on the root, which are the organs that take in nitrogen from the air, which are attached by bacteria. Instead of taking in nitrogen that plants can't use, plants feed carbohydrates to bacteria.

Since these have become clear, many people are seriously thinking about the symbiosis between people and people, and the coexistence between people and nature. The idea is not to think of nature as an enemy, but to live together without injuring but getting the role of each other.

The idea of "symbiosis" is to look at how to help each other, rather than looking at the defects and bad points of each other. The best way of co-existence is when you have someone else, you can do things that you can't do on your own.

Nowadays, it is also considered to coexist with people who are not the leading roles of society, such as people with physical disabilities and seniors. Even those who have difficulty living a normal life can make good use of themselves in the world by coexisting with society. That is also true for children. When children become the conversation partner of seniors, they will become more active. Why don't we all think about what we can do?

Actually, it has recently become clear that the mitochondria (*) in our cells and the chlorophyll possessed by plants originally came from another organism to coexist. Symbiosis may be a very natural thing for organism on the earth.

*Note: Mitochondria; A small organ in the cells of almost all living organisms, with a size of about 0.0005 mm, and on average, 300 to 400 are present in one cell. Generating the energy materials needed to live.

4. Nature

The importance of the "life" of animals and plants

Advances in science and technology have enabled us to reach the bottom of the sea and space. Due to the development of medical science, the average life expectancy is increasing.

However, no matter how much science develops, there are things that cannot be done. It is to create life. There are clones and new creatures born from breeding, but they are creatures that humans have modified the life of nature, not created from scratch.

Humans must not downplay their lives because they cannot create them. Trying to make something that cannot be made or breaking something that can be made is very bad.

On the earth, do you know that a half of the food made by humans is wasted? A half of the food made is scrapped due to the expiration date, leftover food, or no one to buy. Be aware that somewhere in the world there are people who have no food and are dying.

Most of these foods are lives of animals and plants. Not only we waste the effort of the people who made the foods, but we also scrap a half of the lives we cooked to be foods.

Please read more books and listen to the stories of different people to find out much more about the importance of lives on the earth.

Praying

The Japanese have lived with nature since ancient times. Instead of fighting with nature and defeating it, thought to respect nature and live together.

From that way of life, the idea was born that God is present in all things. And in our daily lives, when the sun came up, we put hands together and prayed to the moon begging for rain falls. As such, we have been praying a lot to nature.

With the passage of time, the religion of the world such as Buddhism, Confucianism, Taoism, Christianity, Islam, etc. have been transmitted to the life of the Japanese people in addition to ancient Japanese Shinto. The people of each era of Japan are accepting these nicely and continuing till now.

We have been praying to sky, earth and nature since human power is limited and the heart is easy to wave. Then we can have a strong mind. In the era with little scientific knowledge, natural disasters such as volcanic eruptions, solar eclipses, shooting stars, earthquakes, tsunamis, typhoons, etc. would have been terrifying.

At that time, people have been praying politely to protect their crops. So, praying is the support of our heart born out of human wisdom.

The ancient Shinto tradition in Japan was to give thanks not to ask God. On the other hand, other religions in the world are to ask God or Buddha. We accepted the praying from such foreign countries, thus the hearts of the Japanese people that have continued for 2,000 years can be said to be the hearts gathered from all over the world.

It can be said that it is your mission to connect with the hometown.

Let's save water

About fifteen billion years ago, the universe was about the size of a ball at the beginning. Then a large explosion had occurred that is the big bang. There were hundreds of billions of stars were created in the universe.

At the very beginning of the Kojiki (Japanese oldest historical record), it says, "the name of the god who had appeared to Takamanohara, when the first time to made up of heaven and earth was Ameno-minakanushi-no-kami (The Lord of God in the Universe)"

About 4.5 billion years ago, several planets around the sun were born. The earth is one of them. However, for some reason only the earth had water. It's still not known how it was done. About 1 billion years after that, about 3.5 billion years ago, life was born in the water and organisms appeared. Water has the wonderful power to create life.

You were born after growing in the water called amniotic fluid for about 290 days in your mother's belly.

The Japanese ancestors of the time when Kojiki was written knew the power of water.

Biologically, these 290 days is said to represent the evolutionary processes of the organism since about 3.5 billion years ago. Therefore, water is very important.

That water is now in short all over the world.

Listening to the story, there are people who say, "It's

strange. Since more than a half of the world is the sea". But the water of the sea is seawater, and it cannot be drunk or used for agriculture as it is. It takes a lot of time and energy to remove salt from seawater to make it fresh.

The reason why we are running out of water is that the numbers of humans continue to grow. When the numbers of humans grow, they need food, fuel, and timbers to build houses. For these, we have to develop mountains for creating fields, cut trees for making timbers, and secure places to build houses.

As a result, the mountain becomes a residential area or a bald mountain, reducing its ability to store water. Then, water spattered by rain quickly flows into the sea so that making it difficult for humans to use. Also, wells may dry up and grasslands may become desert.

It seems that many people are thinking that "it's OK to make water when it is necessary", but for example, in order to collect water vapor in the air to make water, the temperature must be lower. It requires energy such as electricity or gas, so if you try to solve the water shortage, you will now have an energy shortage.

When the necessity arises, humans can live without eating for a couple of weeks, but they will die in 4 or 5 days without water. Without water, they won't sweat and won't be able to regulate their body temperature. The toxins that have accumulated inside the body can no longer get out of the body, and the blood flow also deteriorates. And finally, the whole body's functions are damaged and they die.

It is said that there are more than 1 billion people in the world who cannot obtain safe water even though it is so important. There are still many places in the world where a child carries a 20 kilograms jar on the back and goes to carry water for several kilo-meters away.

Now, Japanese people are digging wells around the world. They use Japanese technology to dig a well without using machines so that they can get water safely without bitter experiences. If it spreads, we will solve the water shortages in many of the world.

We are living with water that is ready to drink coming out of the faucet. There are a few countries in the world where drinking tap water does not cause illness, but "we don't want to drink tap water", so Japanese people buy bottled water. What do you think if a child who carries water every day sees us like that?

That's why we want to make a habit to appreciate invisible air and water.

Don't spend too much energy

Energy is needed for moving things, lighting, warming, and making sounds. Energy includes electricity, gas, oil, human and animal power, wind, etc. but the source of all energy is the sun.

For example, in order to generate electricity, we line up solar panels, burn oil or coal, rotate windmills, and use the hydraulic power of dams.

Oil and coal are made from the rays of the sun in the first place, because they were born from plants or animals in ancient era that had been changed under the ground.

The wind that rotates the windmill is generated by the convection of the air warmed by the sunlight.

The water of the dam is the water of the sea that evaporated due to the heat of the sun, which turned into rain and fell onto the upper area of the river.

Considering that, it can be said that the energy we use is given by the sun.

As science develops and our lives become richer, more energy is used. The amount of energy used all over the world is increasing with the pace of doubling in 40 years, and if we continue with this pace, the energy obtained from the sun will not be enough.

The source of underground energy such as oil, coal, natural gas, etc. is the energy stored in the sun for a long time. It can be said that we are now using the heritage of our ancestors more and more. Some people think that it will disappear in the next hundred years.

Another problem is using too much energy. Whenever energy is used, it produces heat, but the heat accumulates and the earth is warmed up. This problem of global warming leads to a terrifying future in which humans may eventually become unable to live. Already, the melting of the Antarctic ice has raised the sea level, and low islands above sea level such as Tuvalu are going to sink into the sea.

It is our desire to live a rich life and to live conveniently and safely, but we need energy to realize it. However, there is a limit to the amount of energy available, and using too much energy can lead to misfortune. If you pursue convenience, the opposite is true. You also have to think carefully about what will happen as a result. We will still have time to prevent it from becoming irreplaceable. Everyone, please study and save this earth.

Do you know the meaning of "recycling"?

We often hear the word "recycling". But can you explain what it means? "Re" means "again", "cycle" means "turning around", and "recycling" means "turning around again" to "use again". It's not to throw away, but about using again.

Now, in your town, when you dispose of garbage, you are doing "separate collection", aren't you? There are some easy ways to separate things such as "burnable trash" and "non-burnable trash", or there are also places where they are sorted by material such as "plastic", "newspaper", "corrugated card-board", and "plastic bottle". There are also ways to separate "burning trash" and "resource trash".

The reason for separating trash is that it is better to recycle. In some towns that are focusing on recycling, some plastic materials are sorted. If they are made of the same material, they can be processed into the next product simply by melting. For example, the fluffy and warm material you wear in winter called fleece is made from plastic bottles.

In more details, there are fellows such as reduce and reuse in recycling, and recycling is also divided into two that are "material recycling" and "thermal recycling".

"Reduce" is to reduce garbage. You can reduce the amount and weight of garbage and lighten the burden of garbage disposal by folding empty boxes or drying raw garbage.

"Reuse" is to use by fixing or cleaning without throwing it away. If you can sell to someone who wants to buy your old bicycles or old clothes, you can save the trash.

"Material recycling" is the use of garbage as a material such as plastic, paper, and metal. It means making clothes from plastic bottles or making cardboard from paper trash.

"Thermal recycling" is a way of thinking that what can only be burned as garbage but cannot be reused is used as fuel. We use the heat of burning garbage to generate electricity and heat up the warm water pool.

Resources will run out in the future. We would like to create a rich world by clever recycling.

Another thing we have to think about is that Japan will become a society where one of four will be senior people. Even now, there are some of seniors who can't open the cap of plastic bottles or the lid of canned coffee. When making products that are easy to recycle, we have to think of products that are easier to use for seniors.

There is no other country in the world like Japan that has been living in harmony with nature and getting along with nature for more than 2,000 years. We Japanese can teach the world how to live richly while caring for things.   By all means, please study these when you have grown up.

Concept of "Mottainai (wasteful)"

There was a person named Ms. Wangari Maathai. A Kenyan woman, for the first time in the world, won the Nobel Peace Prize in the environmental field for her tree planting activities to prevent desertification of the land. When this person came to Japan in 2005, she was impressed to see how Japanese people live. Then she remembered one Japanese word and went home to spread it all over the world. That was the word "Mottainai".

According to Ms. Maathai, "Mottainai" can explain not only all three R's (all start with R in English) of the environmental activities to Reduce, Reuse, and Recycle, but also express Respect.

Ms. Maathai thought about making "Mottainai" a universal word and started promoting it. Unfortunately, Ms. Maathai died of cancer in 2011, but her thought was succeeded to the former Brazilian Minister of the Environment, Ms. Marina Silva, and it has become a global movement.

Originally, "Mottai" was written as "importance" and it was a Buddhism word. It means weightily and with "not", "Mottainai" means "the real value is not recognized". From that point on, the feeling of "being treated poorly and it is regrettable" came to be included, and the word was changed to "Mottainai," which is the current world word.

Ms. Wangari Maathai started the "Mottainai Campaign" throughout the world through the UN Women's empowerment committee and Rescue Africa Live with world musicians. After that, Ms. Maathai often visited Japan and gave a lecture at "Mottainai National Convention" to spread the spirit of "Mottainai" to Japanese people once again. Due to her such achievements, Ms. Maathai received a national medal from the Japanese government in 2009.

In Japan, many activities such as "Mt. Fuji Garbage Pickup Tournament", "Mottainai Flea Market", "Mottainai Kids Flea Market", "Mottainai Green Project", and "Mottainai Handicraft Market" etc. are being carried out. One word of Japan has been transmitted to the world, and it has come back to Japan as a big movement.

As a source country of "Mottainai", we must actively promote and spread the spirit of "Mottainai".

Then, after "Mottainai", it is the turn of "Shitsuke" into a world word. It has already spread in China, South Korea, Taiwan and Mongolia.

Blessings of nature and disasters

Nature gives us a lot of blessings, but sometimes it brings great disasters. The Great East Japan Earthquake, known as "3.11", caused damage to nearly 20,000 people, only just the dead and missing.

Not only earthquakes, but nature often hits us. Typhoons, heavy rain, heavy snow, floods, high tides, Tsunamis, eruptions, etc. Each time these destroyed people's lives and caused damages, these are reminded of how weak humans are.

In Japan, children used to list up scary things like "earthquake, thunder, fire, and father" since long time ago. Children were much more scared of natural disasters than angry fathers.

No matter how much people proud of a computer or the Internet, if the electric wires are cut at many points and the electricity stops, it will be useless. Even if you have a fine car, if the road becomes unusable, it is a useless treasure.

The old people were much more humble about nature than we are now. Instead of saying, "I can freely handle nature", they humbled themselves, "I want to live in harmony with nature", or "I want to take care of nature". They never thought that "I can rule nature freely".

Natural disasters that sometimes overwhelm us may be nature's punishment for us humans, who have swelled head and destroyed nature.

"Human doesn't have much power. If you look at nature stupidly by taking it lightly, it will be a serious result", that may be the message of a landslip or a flood. Why don't you think again?

No matter how advanced human technologies are, we cannot completely stop natural disasters. But please study and research from these natural disasters before becoming a waste, think those as research data, understand them as soon as possible, and to be the least damage rather than stop them.

It is human ability that cannot even divert the course of a Typhoon, and does not know when an earthquake will occur. Rather, it is better to think of "what humans can do is limited" and to prepare for natural disasters by thinking "it must happen".

Always keep a humble attitude without acting arrogantly. This is the attitude you may need to take for everything, not just for nature.

Human tragedy usually comes from arrogance.
Old people said.
"A natural disaster comes when we forgot it."

Let's feel the great beauty of nature more

Even if you're surrounded by wonderful things, you start to feel it is normal, and you can't feel the greatness. This is the habit of human beings.

The human brain has the special feature that if you look at the same thing, you will get bored. This is necessary for progress and growth, but it also has the side effect of lightly looking at the important things.

What we must never forget is the splendor of nature. When we see the green landscape in the morning sun, our brains are very active. But if you think that it's "Atarimae (as usual)", that activity will be slowed down.

However, it is said that the most of children in these days don't see the sunrise. This is a problem because the human brain is supposed to be switched on when seeing the morning sun.

Blessing of nature and the splendor of nature cannot be created by human power. Humans cannot create the sun, the earth, the plants, the mountains, the sea, etc. by our own power. Of course, there are no living beings that humans can create. However, humans can protect nature. Let's think about what we should protect in the nature.

 It is human beings who go to hiking and says "Surely enough, nature is good", but also saying that "We want to come by car more conveniently" and builds a road by crushing hills and fields. We tend to think that there is still so much nature, so we wonder if it would be okay to reduce it a little.

Or you may be thinking, "It will be OK if it's only me".

However, the lost nature is not completely restored. It's too late after it's gone. If all people, from children to adults, don't think "let's preserve nature" and "protect nature", the nature that humans feel comfortable will be lost more and more from this earth.

We assume that you've all seen pictures of Mars or Moon, don't you? Did you think it was wonderful nature? It's the world where humans cannot live without wearing space suits. That is the nature of Mars and Moon.

There are countless stars in the universe, but humans have not yet found a star with the same nature as Earth. Maybe there isn't one. It is important to remember that our earth is so precious and we would like to consider it deeply.

The visible and the invisible things

There are two types of things in this world. It is "visible" and "invisible".

What is visible is something that can be felt by your body or touched by your hands such as pencils, erasers, desks and books. Simply, it is a "thing".

Invisible things are things such as words, feelings, and hearts, that its presence is clear but it cannot be touched by our hands or have no shape. Also a soul or a ghost may be in the same category.

Old people treated what visible and invisible as the same. They respected the gods and ancestors, visited the grave and put hands together. When they came to the shrine, they thanked with two bows, two hand claps, and one bow.

They thought that "ghosts and monsters maybe exist".

But people now are no longer value invisible things. It's because only things that can be measured in shape, size, and weight are considered to be "things in this world" after the advancement of science. Things that can't be expressed in numbers are seen with special eyes as "religion" or "occult". And if we say, "Our heart is important", they will return, "Then, show me your heart in front of me".

As a result, greetings and courtesy have been forgotten. At many homes, it is now becoming to the custom of eating meals without saying "Itadakimasu". Saying "Good morning" and "Good night" has decreased among families. On the contrary, since each person acts at his or her own free time, it is not unusual for the family not to meet even in the same house.

However, we can never be happy if you only value what you can see because your life is invisible. If we judge human beings only by what we can see, it means that a person with good style and nice looking is a great person. But this is not the case.

By all means, please have the idea of "making invisible things important". If you do so, your heart will be surely brushed up to have a right mind and you will live a happy life.

From now on, let's make a habit of thinking about the difference between what is visible and what is not visible every day. Then you can really understand what's important.

Universe and humans

We think that you will learn a lot of knowledge by going to junior high school and high school. For example, you will learn that, "things" are made of molecules, and the molecules are made of atoms. There are protons, electrons, and neutrons in one atom, and the electrons are running around the cluster of protons and neutrons. That is the true nature of everything, and the universe is the collection of these.

A mysterious thing created in such a world of "things" that is the "creatures". Creatures act by themselves and increase their families. This is impossible in a world of "things" only.

Then why "living things" were created? We don't know why. It was created by chances are piled up with chances. So far, that is the most belief thinking.

The latest scientific research explores the small world, one billionth meter, called nanometer. Using what they have learned, they are developing technology called nanotechnology that manipulates atoms and molecules to create new materials and invisible size of machines.

These are difficult for elementary school students, but there is a picture book called "What is Nano? ~Adventure of Benji and Bruno~" written by Dr. Harry Kroto of England, who won the Nobel Prize, written for Japanese children. If you see it in the school library, please be sure to read it.

We tend to think that science today is universal, but what we really know by science is only a small part of the world.

In front of the mysteries of the universe, we humans are tiny presence. Let's live every day while feeling that surely. It's small, but the only shining presence in the universe, that is you.

【本書は『しあわせに生きる』(2011年初版、冨山房インターナショナル発行)の英語版です】

For Happy Life

─────────────────────────────────────

2020年11月6日　第1刷発行

編　者　　一般社団法人日本躾の会

訳　者　　唐　澤　　豊

発行者　　坂　本　喜　杏

発行所　　株式会社冨山房インターナショナル
　　　　　〒101-0051
　　　　　東京都千代田区神田神保町1-3
　　　　　TEL　03(3291)2578　FAX　03(3219)4866
　　　　　URL　www.fuzambo-intl.com

印　刷　　株式会社冨山房インターナショナル

製　本　　加藤製本株式会社

─────────────────────────────────────